I0820436

Words that are tricky to understand are in **bold.** Find out what they mean in the glossary.

Words that are difficult to say are in *italics.* Find out how to say them at the back of the book.

ARE SPIDER WEBS STRONGER THAN STEEL?

DISCOVER THE SCIENCE BEHIND ***ARACHNOLOGY***
(ah-RACK-noh-luh-jee)

Written by Olivia Watson
Illustrated by Valeria Abatzoglu

WHAT IS ARACHNOLOGY?

Arachnology is the scientific study of *arachnids* – a group of animals which includes spiders, scorpions, and **harvestmen**.

The scientists who study arachnology are called **ARACHNOLOGISTS.**

Around the world, spiders are lurking in bushes, trees, and buildings, spinning webs and weaving traps ready to catch unsuspecting **prey**. Their secret weapon? The delicate, yet powerful, threads of silk they use to make their webs, which can be both sticky and strong!

Humans have known for thousands of years that spider silk is incredibly strong. Ancient groups of people used it to close up **wounds,** and some even used it to make fishing lines! But what makes spider silk so strong? That's something modern *arachnologists* are trying to figure out...

To answer that question, scientists have to decide what it means to be strong. There are many ways to measure strength. Some animals have great lifting power, like dung beetles which can move things more than 1,000 times their body weight!

Some animals have powerful bites, like saltwater crocodiles which can easily chomp through muscles and bones with their teeth.

Other animals have squeezing strength, like kingsnakes which use their powerful bodies to hold onto, and completely crush, their prey!

Spider silk can have lots of **tensile strength** – it can be stretched and pulled an extreme amount without breaking. This helps certain spider **species** wrap up and hold onto prey so tightly that escape is impossible.

The silk of some orb weavers is so strong it can hold animals **much bigger than insects!**

Spiders don't just use their webs for catching prey – they also use them to get around! Some spiders create parachutes out of their webs. When they get caught by the wind, the spiders are carried huge distances. Their silky webs can carry them across oceans to remote islands before breaking!

To understand the power of spider silk, arachnologists had to look closer. By studying silk under powerful microscopes, they discovered it's not one big strand, but lots of tiny strands – each thinner than a human hair.

Most spiders twist the silk strands together. But the brown recluse's silk strands run side by side. This spider occasionally adds little loops which seems to make their silk even stronger.

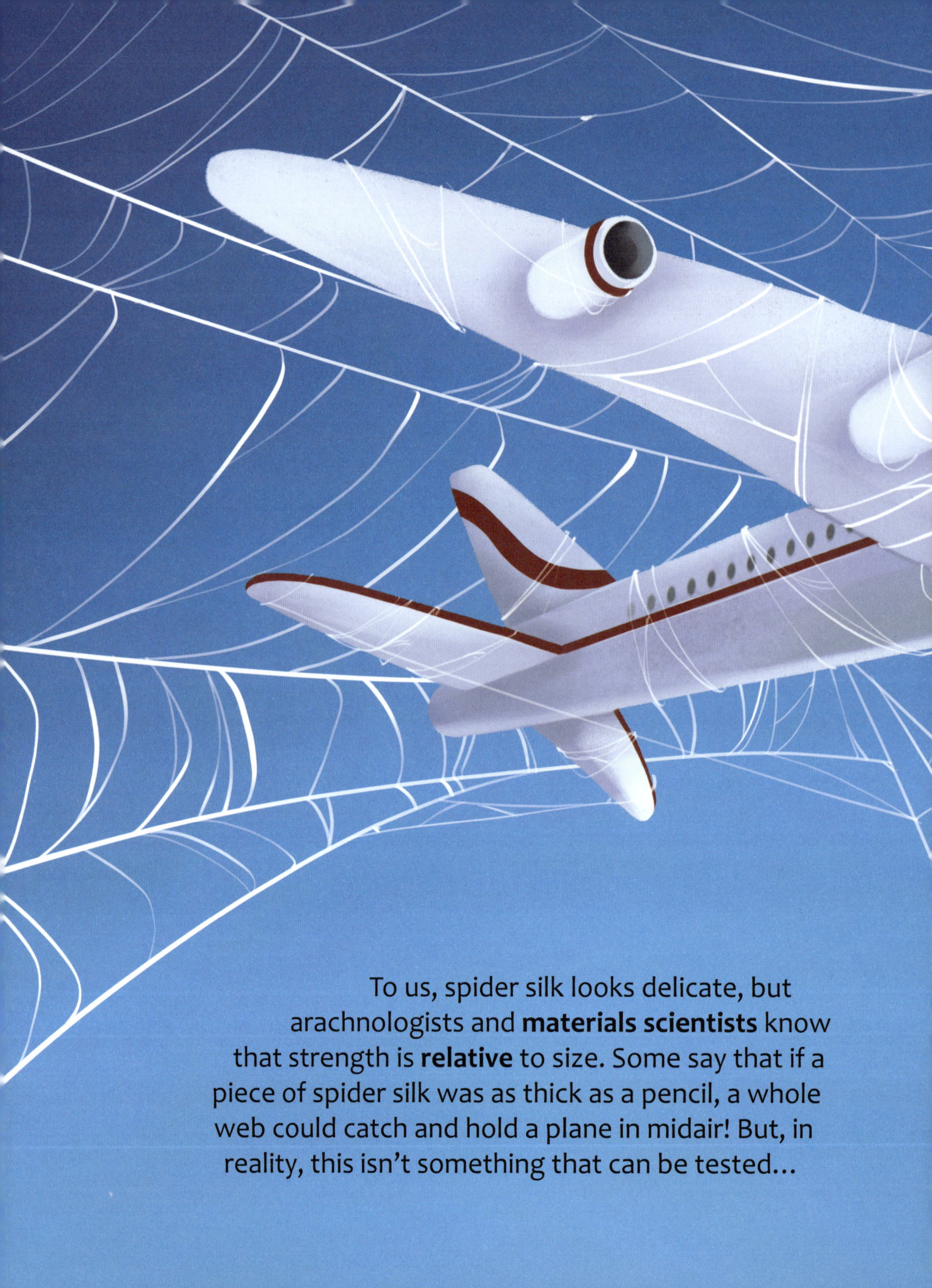

To us, spider silk looks delicate, but arachnologists and **materials scientists** know that strength is **relative** to size. Some say that if a piece of spider silk was as thick as a pencil, a whole web could catch and hold a plane in midair! But, in reality, this isn't something that can be tested…

But scientists have done some important experiments. They wanted to compare spider silk with strong **human-made** materials, like steel, that are used to build bridges and skyscrapers.

Cutting steel to the same thickness as spider silk led to an incredible discovery – on this scale, spider silk is five times stronger, making it one of **the world's toughest materials!**

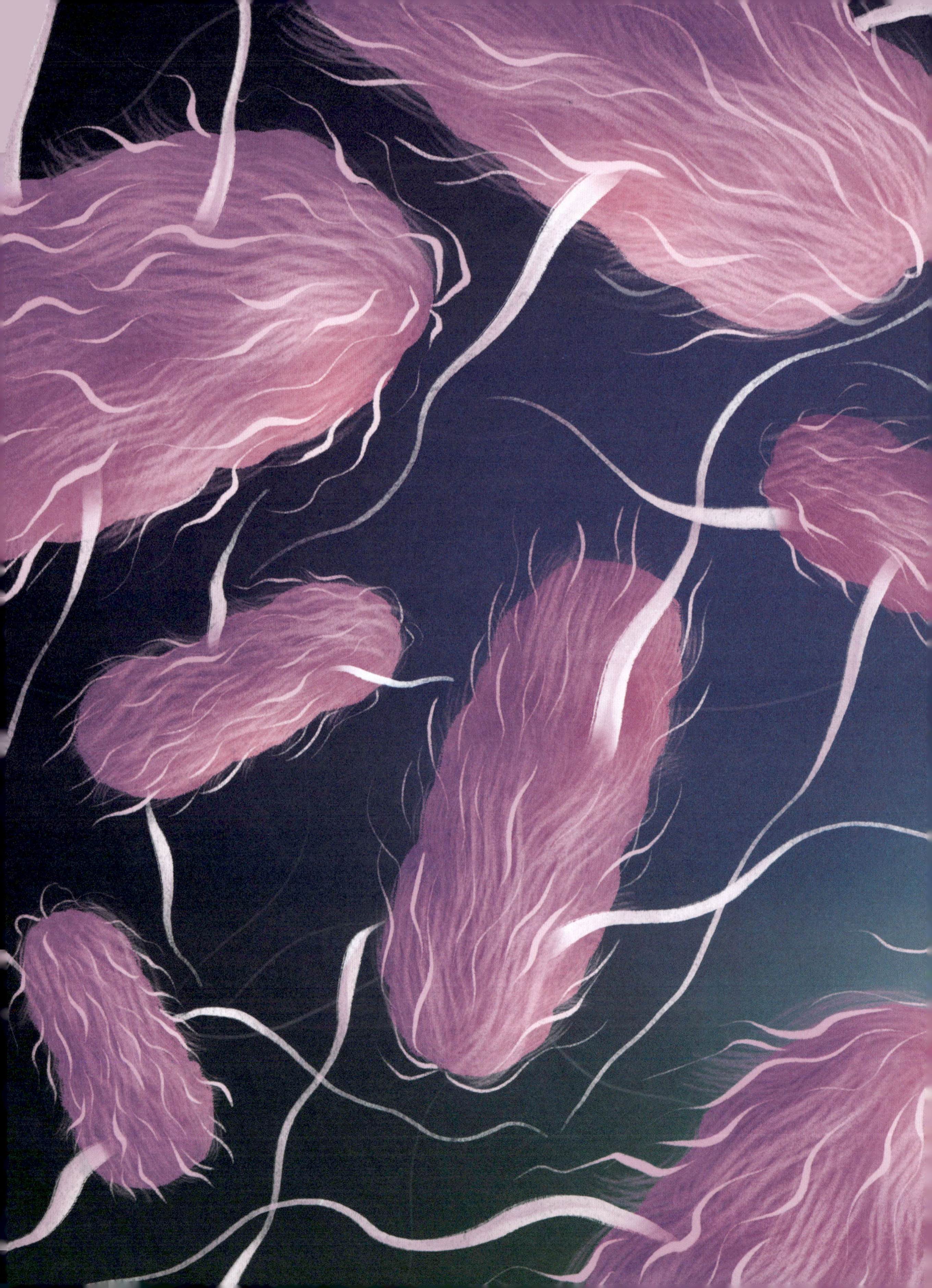

Because it's so light, small, and strong, scientists call spider silk a "**supermaterial**"! They think it could be used in many interesting ways, but it's too difficult to **harvest** from spiders on a big scale. It's taken years, but they've found a way to make their own spider silk,

with some help from bacteria!

Recreating spider silk on a big scale means it can be used to make all sorts of items. It's already being turned into clothes and shoes, but some scientists are taking this one step further. They have made silk that could be used to create important safety clothing that's **tougher than protective vests!**

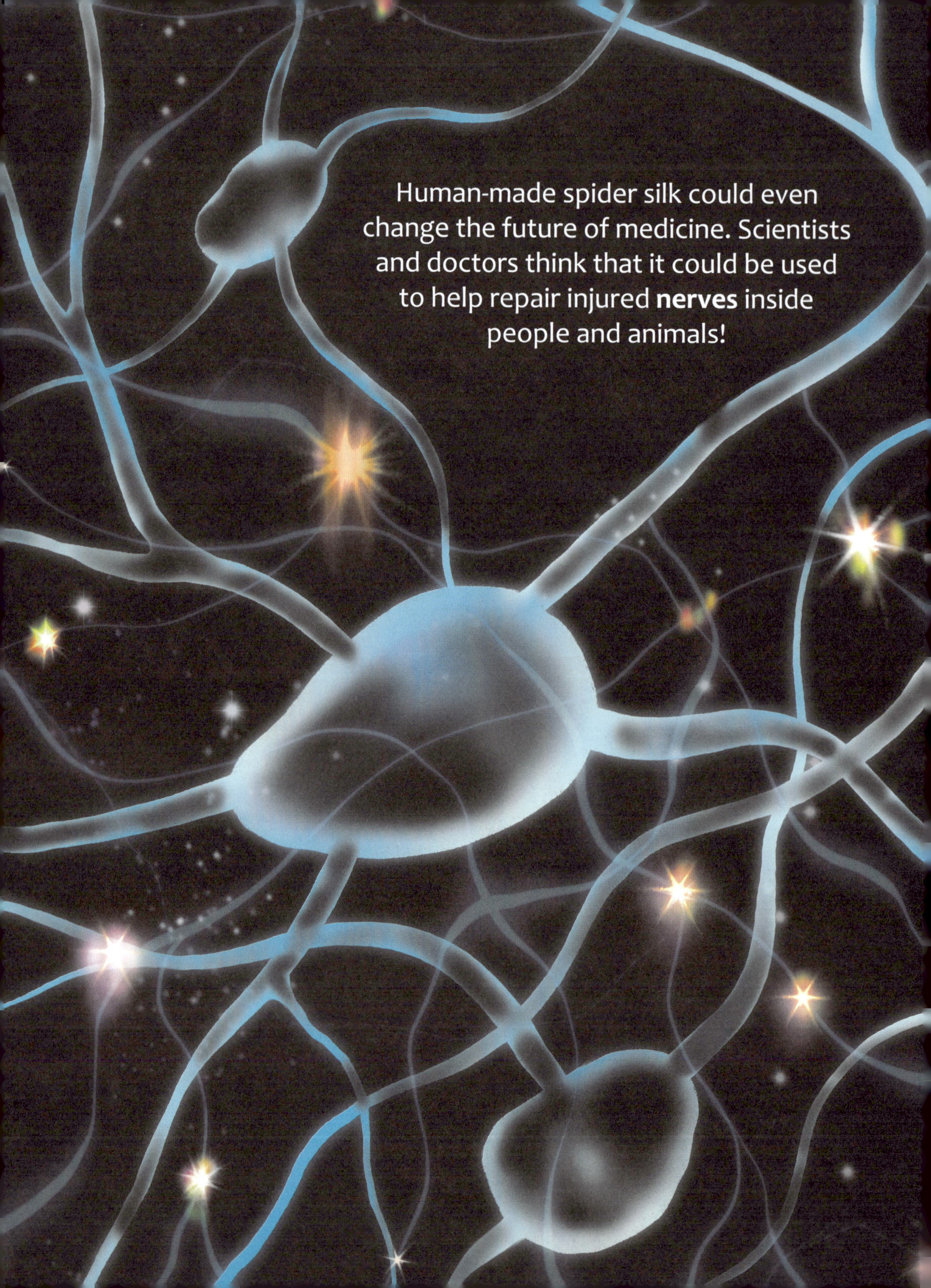

Human-made spider silk could even change the future of medicine. Scientists and doctors think that it could be used to help repair injured **nerves** inside people and animals!

The silk would act like a guide for nerve **cells** to grow across, its strength and flexibility helping the body repair itself. It could heal wounds in the same way, allowing skin and damaged **tissue** to regrow.

But what we know about spider webs won't just help our bodies, but the whole world! Scientists have made tiny sensors by **modifying** real spider silk. These sensors can be printed on almost anything, even flowers! They send back information about nature, which helps scientists keep our planet healthy.

Web-spinning spiders have led scientists to fascinating discoveries about how strong their silk really is. While spider silk could strengthen metals, like those used in buildings and bridges, to make them tougher, it isn't big or stiff enough to hold up these heavy things on its own.

So, although spider webs are strong and impressive in many ways, they'll never completely replace steel!

Weird and wonderful

SPIDER WEBS

Spider silk is incredibly strong, but what does it look like in the wild? Different spiders weave their webs differently. Here are some wicked web styles scientists have found.

ORB WEBS

These webs are some of the most iconic! They are circular with straight lines coming out from the middle, a bit like a bicycle wheel.

SHEET WEBS

Sheet webs are thin, flat, and horizontal. They're found on grass, low plants, and soil. Some people call these types of webs "hammock webs" because of how they look from the side!

FUNNEL WEBS

Some spiders build funnel-shaped webs to live inside. These look like deep, dark tunnels and they are often found in the corners of buildings or thick plants and deep places in nature.

TRIP WIRES

Sometimes funnel-shaped webs have extra lines of silk around the tunnel entrance. These act like trip wires, alerting the spider to nearby prey so it can rush out and catch it!

WEB DECORATION

Certain spiders decorate their webs with zig zags! Scientists aren't sure why, but they think it might help with **camouflaging** the spider, attracting prey, or adding strength to the web.

Spin-credible

SPIDER FACTS

There's so much to discover about the world of arachnology. Do you know the answers to some of the world's biggest questions about spiders?

HOW MANY DIFFERENT SPIDERS ARE THERE?

Scientists have discovered more than 50,000 arachnid species! They all produce silk, but they don't all make webs.

HOW LONG HAVE SPIDERS BEEN AROUND?

The earliest known spiders appeared over 300 million years ago. Many of them belonged to the group *Mesothelae*, which still has living relatives in parts of Asia today.

DO SPIDERS HAVE GOOD SENSES?

Spiders have up to eight eyes, but they don't all have good eyesight. Many rely on vibrations, touch, and taste to get around, catch their prey, and spot **mates** or rivals.

ARE SPIDERS DANGEROUS?

Some spiders are harmless, but others are really bad news! The Sydney funnel-web is one of the most **venomous** spiders in the world. Its bite can be deadly if not treated fast enough.

DO SPIDERS LIVE ON THEIR OWN?

Yes! Most spiders live alone, but this isn't always the case. Some spiders live in colonies of thousands of individual spiders, working together to catch prey. These are called "social spiders".

GLOSSARY

Bacteria – tiny living things that can be found in all natural environments.

Camouflaging – the way animals blend in with their surroundings so they can't be seen easily.

Cells – the smallest parts of a living thing.

Harvest – to gather or collect a plant or animal product.

Harvestmen – a group of spider-like arachnids with very long and thin legs.

Human-made – something that is made by humans.

Materials scientists – scientists who study the properties and uses of different materials.

Mates – one of a pair of animals that live or have babies together.

Modifying – changing something for a specific reason.

Nerves – thin, string-like parts of the body that carry messages between the brain and other body parts.

Prey – an animal that is hunted by other animals for food.

Relative – comparing something based on two factors. For example, comparing something's strength with its size.

Species – a group of living things that share characteristics and features, and produce young together. For example, brown recluse and Chilean recluse spiders are different species.

Supermaterial – a material with extraordinary properties.

Tensile strength – the amount of stress a material can stand when pulled or stretched before breaking.

Tissue (body tissue) – a group of cells (see left) that perform a specific task inside the body, like muscles.

Venomous – a creature that produces venom to hurt or kill their prey (see left).

Wounds – injuries to the skin.

HOW DO I SAY?

Arachnids
ah-RACK-nidz

Arachnology
ah-RACK-noh-luh-jee

Arachnologists
ah-RACK-noh-luh-jists

Mesothelae
meh-zuh-THEE-lay

THE BIG QUESTIONS ANSWERED

This is more than just a series of books; it is a complete resource. Accompanying each book is a variety of FREE material to engage curious kids with science.

www.thebigquestionsanswered.com

Use the QR code to visit the website, download free resources, and discover other books in the series.

On the website, find out incredible things about arachnologists, including what they do, some of their greatest discoveries, and the people who have made a difference in this field of science.

The material is also available for home or classroom use, supporting all the information in this book.

Teachers' & Parents' Resources
With discussion prompts, questions, and extra information around key topics.

Activity Pack
Fun activities including creative writing, word searches, and more.

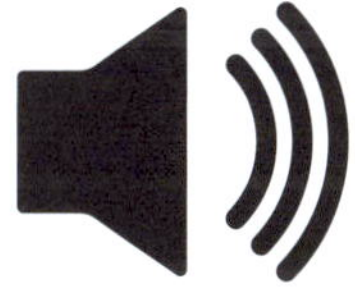

Audio Book
Experience this book in audio, narrated by a professional voice actor.

The Big Questions Answered is published by Beetle Books.
Beetle Books is an imprint of Hungry Tomato Ltd.

First published in 2025 by Hungry Tomato Ltd
F15, Old Bakery Studios, Blewetts Wharf, Malpas Road,
Truro, Cornwall, TR1 1QH, UK.

ISBN 9781835691519

A CIP catalog record for this book is available from the British Library.

With thanks to:
Editors: Holly Thornton and Jenny Rowan
Designers: Meg Holbrook and Amy Harvey
The team at Beehive Illustration
Consultant: Professor Sara Goodacre

Information in this book is up to date as of the time of writing.

Printed and bound in China.

Picture Credits:
(t = top, b = bottom, m = middle, l = left, r = right)
Shutterstock: Adeel Ahmed photos 32ml; IanRedding 32br; Ken Griffiths 35mr; Mark Breck 33ml; Md Aziman 33br; NNphotos 33tr; Pixel-Shot 34mr; Lukas Jonaitis 35tl; Tomasz Klejdysz 35bl.

Wikipedia: By Marshal Hedin - https://www.flickr.com/photos/23660854@N07/21260158468/in/photolist-yoFSqm-xJg35f-kTSF1H-nNErBR, CC BY-SA 34bl.